This Journal Belongs To:

_____

Possibility Begins When You Believe
Tomorrow can be Different from Today.
Possibility is an Action that Must be Taken
Every Single Day. Today is Just the Start...

Hello Possibility...

Made in the USA
Middletown, DE
10 June 2022

66957400R00071